Contents

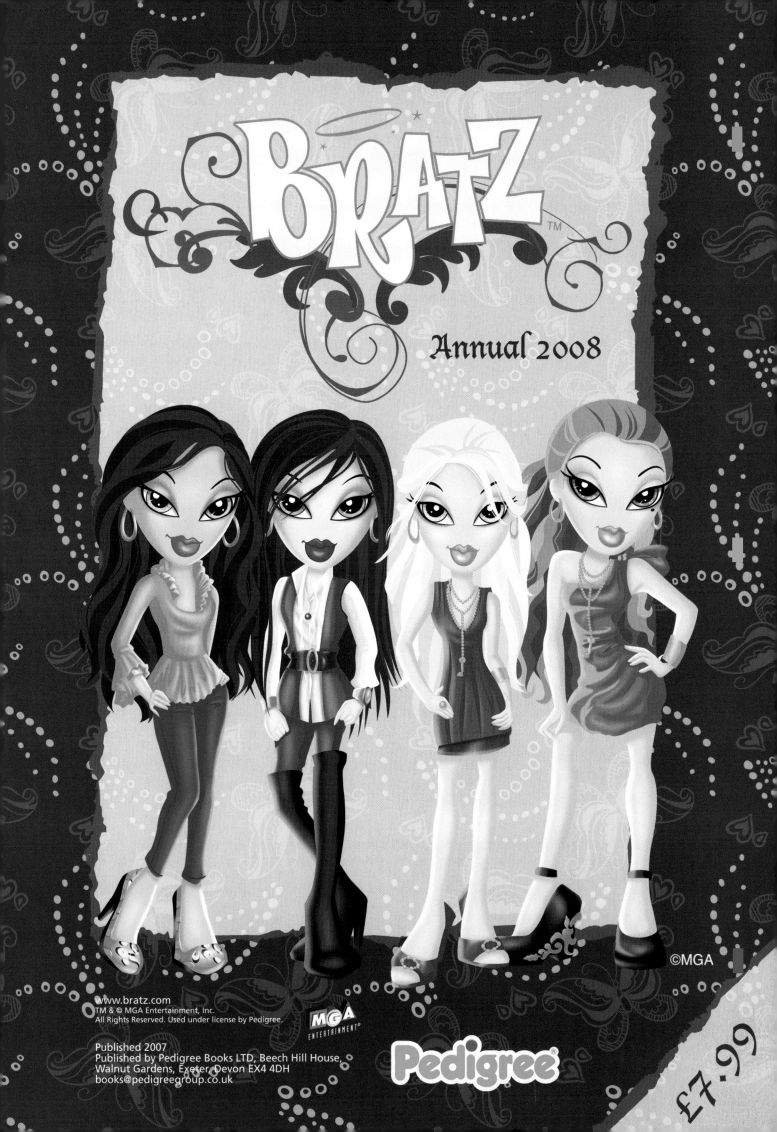

Annual 2008

©MGA

£7.99

MGA
ENTERTAINMENT®

Published 2007
Published by Pedigree Books LTD, Beech Hill House,
Walnut Gardens, Exeter, Devon EX4 4DH
books@pedigreegroup.co.uk

Pedigree®

Cloe

© MGA

Come and meet the best-dressed Angel in town! Cloe's super-inspired by art, and she sees everything with the eyes of a true artist.

When she's not designing fantastic fashions with her best friends, she's creating cool new cosmetic looks that belong on the hottest catwalks!

She's a total drama queen, but her friends love her and she sure keeps life exciting.

With Cloe around, there's always an adventure waiting to happen!

© MGA

Sneak Peek Profile

Nickname: Angel.
Fave Colour: Turquoise.
Lucky Number: 6.
Fave Movies: Big epics.
Fave Books: Mysteries
Music Inspiration: Hilary Duff!
Fave Class: Art.
Fashion Passion: Dramatic diva clothes!
Shoppin' Style: Beauty products and glittering makeup.
Hollywood Inspiration: Cameron Diaz.

Jade

Always laid back and utterly cutting-edge, Jade's definitely the Kool Kat on the block.

She has the inside track on the hottest trends, and she has an eye for style that all her friends admire.

Jade is always one step ahead of the game, but she is totally generous with her gift and she often snags new outfits for her best friends while she's scoping out boutiques!

Sneak Peek Profile

Nickname: Kool Kat.
Fave Colour: Green.
Lucky Number: 11.
Fave Movies: Edgy foreign films from ultra-modern directors.
Fave Books: I prefer fashion mags!
Music Inspiration: Gwen Stefani.
Fave Class: Chemistry - I love the mix of cool science and creative theory!
Fashion Passion: Anything new and quirky-cool.
Shoppin' Style: The coolest shops and the hippest styles.
Hollywood Inspiration: Jessica Alba.

Yasmin

Yasmin is the quietest of the four friends, because she likes to sit back and reflect before she speaks. Because of that, she gives awesome advice!

Her gentle nature makes everyone love her!

Yasmin's always interested in alternative trends and does a ton of work for charity.

© MGA

Sneak Peek Profile

Nickname: Pretty Princess.
Fave Colour: Forest green.
Lucky Number: 7.
Fave Movies: Romantic comedies.
Fave Books: Chick-lit with happy endings.
Music Inspiration: Cold Play.
Fave Class: Creative writing.
Fashion Passion: Blending different styles into a graceful glam look.
Shoppin' Style: Bargain hunter.
Hollywood Inspiration: Kate Winslet.

Sasha™

Sasha knows who she is, what she wants and how to get it!

Music is a huge part of her life, and she always has the lowdown on the latest and greatest sounds and bands.

Sometimes she can come across as a little bossy, but her friends love her upfront style and really value her plain speaking - most of the time!

Sneak Peek Profile

Nickname: Bunny Boo.
Fave Colour: Violet.
Lucky Number: 3.
Fave Movies: Comedy dramas.
Fave Books: Autobiographies of people I admire.
Music Inspiration: Beyoncé.
Fave Class: Dance.
Fashion Passion: Street style - anything funky!
Shoppin' Style: Fast and furious!
Hollywood Inspiration: Angelina Jolie.

Meygan™

Meygan's always on the hunt for a new adventure, whether it's travelling to a new land or trying out something new right here at home.

She keeps in touch with all the friends she's made while travelling, and they help her keep up with the latest exotic chic trends!

Meygan's always ready to take a walk on the wild side!

14

Sneak Peek Profile

Nickname: Funky Fashion Monkey.
Fave Colour: Cinnamon.
Lucky Number: 19.
Fave Movies: Animations.
Fave Books: Spy novels.
Music Inspiration: The Black-Eyed Peas!
Fave Class: Yoga class (after school!).
Fashion Passion: Sprucin' up a humdrum outfit with a touch of the exotic like an animal-print scarf.
Shoppin' Style: I love to travel and pick up new pieces from different places.
Hollywood Inspiration: Scarlett Johanssen.

15

YOUR WORLD
NOW WE WANT TO FIND OUT ABOUT YOU!

1 Grab your camera or mobile phone, and go for a walk around your neighbourhood. Take snaps of your house, your friends' houses, your school – and everything else that is important in your life. You're gonna map out your world, so think about the shops, your youth club, your dance class … and don't forget to sneak a shot of the house where your crush lives!

2 When you have a collection of photos, gather together everything you will need to create your awesome life map. Don't forget glue, some soft colouring pencils and a gorgeous pen.

3 Stick a pic of your house in the space at the centre of the map. This is the most important part of the map!

4 Draw lines from your house to create a map of your neighbourhood. Add your friends' houses to the map and then use the soft pencils to draw a border around the photos in your fave colour. Keep adding photos until all the important places you snapped are on the map.

Take some photos of your best friends and stick them around the edge of the map to create an awesome border!

From each photo, carefully draw a speech bubble, just like the one that comes from the photo of your house. Fill in each speech bubble with fun facts and secret info. Tell us all about your best friends and why they are so cool. Describe your school and write down your best and worst lessons! Don't forget to tell us all about your crush!

© MGA

HOT TIP :: If you need more space, create your map on a big piece of coloured cardboard. Head down to your local craft shop and ask for a sheet of A2 cardboard in your fave colour.

Think about what makes your home so great, and stick extras onto your map. You could choose cinema tickets, pressed flowers or flyers for the hottest DJs. Label everything you stick into the book. When your map is finished, dab small spots of glue across the page, then sprinkle glitter onto it.

SUDOKU QUEEN

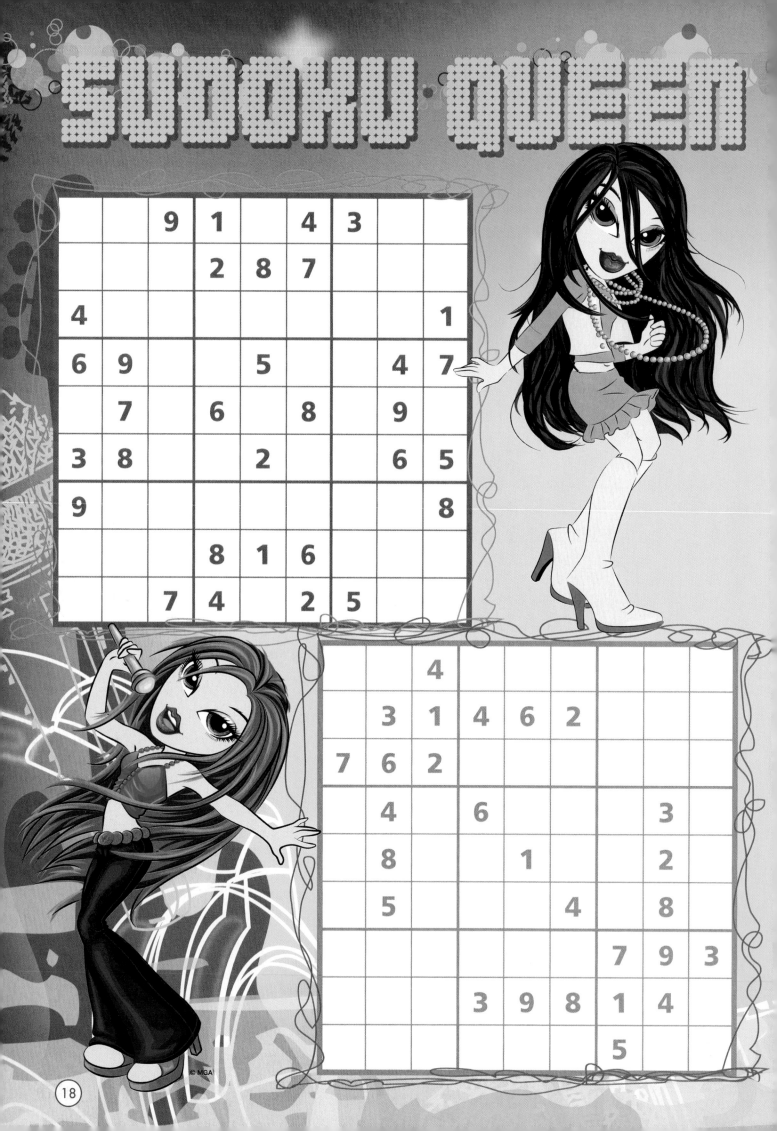

DO YOU SUDOKU? HERE ARE FOUR PUZZLES TO TRY OUT ? SO GET BUSY AND CHALLENGE YOURSELF. TIME HOW LONG EACH PUZZLE TAKES YOU AND SEE IF YOU CAN IMPROVE YOUR TIME!

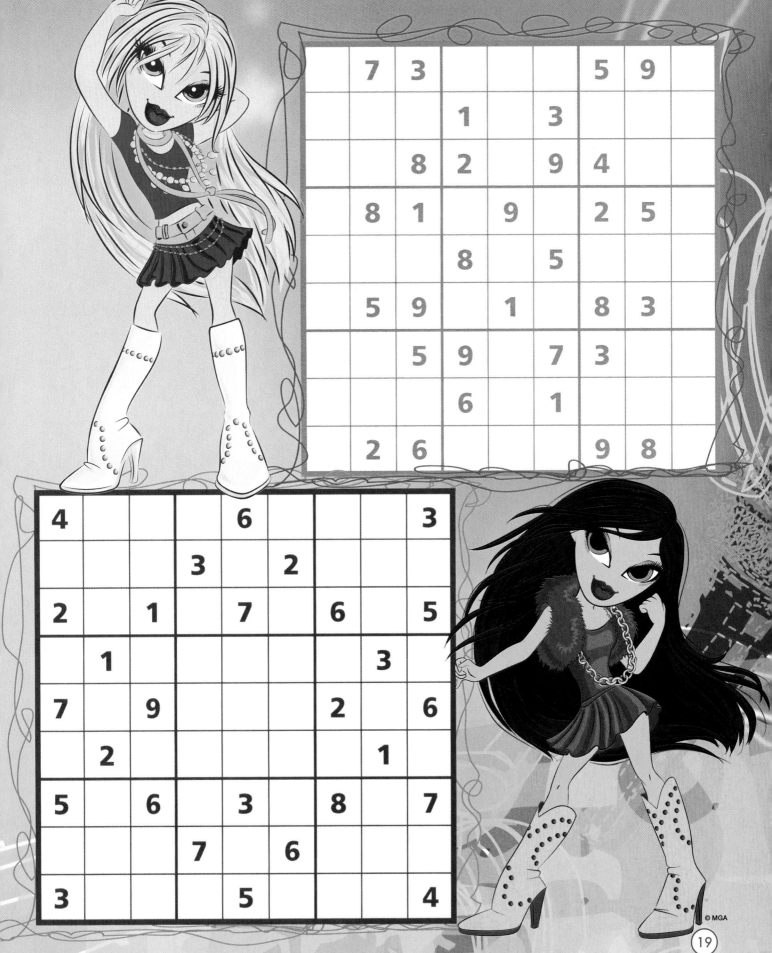

© MGA

Brilliant Bags

What do you keep in your bag? Is it organised and neat like Sasha's, or a glorious mish-mash of notes and fabric pieces like Jade's? However you use your bag, here are our essentials for the perfect accessory!

Phone

Keys

Purse

Sunnies

Compact umbrella

Mini vaporiser filled with your fave perfume for a quick spritz

Notebook and pen for jotting down inspiring ideas!

Mini brush

Mini concealer / all-in-one makeup

Lip balm

Emery board

A busy girl needs to have essentials at her fingertips. She also needs to be able to react quickly in a makeup or nail emergency!

As every fashionista knows, one bag is just not enough! Different bags suit different outfits, so the contents of your bag need to be easy to move!

Clean out your bags regularly. You can even use a vacuum cleaner to suck up all those bits that gather at the bottom!

Remember, keep it small and compact! Only carry things you will often need, and don't use your bag as a rubbish bin. Having to disentangle your hairbrush from gum wrappers is not cool!

© MGA

Some people seem to look totally stylin' in any hat, but most of us suit some styles more than others! If you love hats but think you can't wear them, check out our tips and think again!

If you have a high forehead or a long face, choose snugly fitting hats to help frame your face. Look for a high brim that lifts up to show off your face.

If you have a low forehead or a round face, go for a taller hat with the brim dipping slightly over one eye for film-star appeal!

Next time you're heading to a family wedding, accessorise a floaty, feminine with a feathery mini-hat for an utterly glam vibe.

A large brimmed hat is super glam, or you can complete a casual look with a funky beanie.

The crown of your hat should never be narrower than your cheekbones.

Always choose your hat after you've picked your outfit. If your outfit is glam and eye-poppin', go for a simple hat. If your outfit is understated and elegant, your hat can be more dressy!

If you are still nervous about wearing a hat, go for a flower hairband or hairclip. They look fabulous in your hair and will help you get used to the look of something on your head.

Hot Hats!

Jade latest tip is that hats are coming back big time! Years ago every glam girl finished off her outfit with a hat, and now that ultra-stylin' retro look is getting a modern edge!

21

DREAM DIARY

Do you remember your dreams? Most people don't, but they can be a great way to make sense of things that are worrying you. If you don't know what to do about a certain situation, you might just find the answers in your dreams!

Your dreams are totally unique – just like your fashion style! They send you messages using symbols. If you start keeping a dream diary, it will help you to figure out what all the symbols mean!

:: Keep your dream diary next to your bed. As soon as you wake up, write down :: everything you can remember about your dreams.

:: Every time you think you have worked out a symbol, write that down too. :: Remember, people can be symbols as well!

:: As you get into the habit of writing down your dreams, :: you will start to remember them better.

:: When you have filled up these pages, carry on in a special, secret, dream notebook! ::

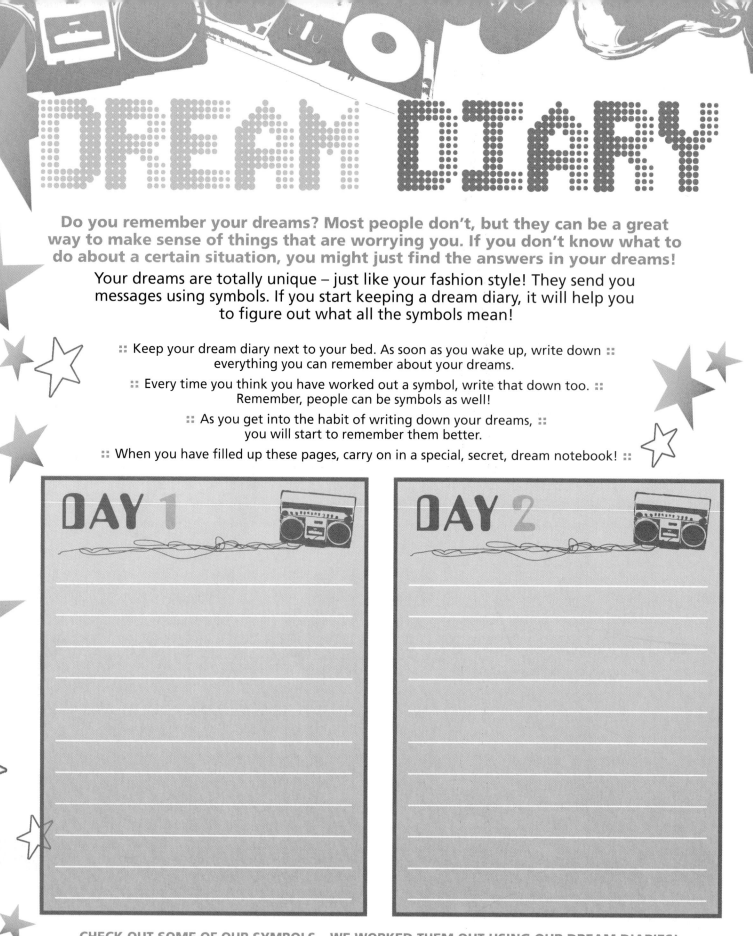

DAY 1

DAY 2

CHECK OUT SOME OF OUR SYMBOLS – WE WORKED THEM OUT USING OUR DREAM DIARIES!
When Jade dreams about polka dots, she knows they are a symbol of something she can't bear!
Cloe's dreams are always full of the colour blue when she's really happy.
For Yasmin, pens symbolise ideas!
When Sasha feels confused, she dreams that her wardrobe is as disorganised as Jade's!

DAY 3

_____
_____
_____
_____
_____
_____
_____
_____

DAY 4

_____
_____
_____
_____
_____
_____
_____
_____

DAY 5

_____
_____
_____
_____
_____
_____
_____
_____
_____
_____

DAY 6

_____
_____
_____
_____
_____
_____
_____
_____
_____
_____

DAY 7

_____
_____
_____
_____
_____
_____
_____
_____

MY SYMBOLS

_____
_____
_____
_____
_____
_____
_____

MEYGAN'S LIPS TIPS

Everyone loves a smiling face, and it's your most natural accessory! Here are my fave tips to making the most of your smile!

Dry, cracking lips are not cool! Find a lip balm that really suits your lips and carry it with you everywhere.

PROBLEM:
Thin lips.

Beauty SOS!

INSTANT SOLUTION:
Brush a damp, soft toothbrush gently over your lips for 30 seconds.

24

© MGA

Beauty SOS!

Chew on some parsley sprigs!

Use a whitening toothpaste to help keep your teeth gleaming!

When you're brushing your teeth, brush your tongue too. Bacteria can live on your tongue and they cause bad breath.

Floss your teeth daily – it will keep them looking fabulous and it will make going to the dentist even less of a chore!

Check out the various lip plumpers that are on the market at the moment – they are a great temporary solution and can have a totally awesome and fun effect!

Perfect your pout! Look at those old-style glam pics of Marilyn Monroe and think gorgeous!

Stunning lips need gleaming teeth to set them off. Make sure you visit the dentist twice a year for a checkup and clean. There's nothing to be scared of.

If you need a brace, don't panic. There are tons of celebs who have worn braces – and they have the perfect teeth to prove it! Seriously, it might seem like a total nightmare at first. But girl, when that brace comes off you are going to have a smile that will dazzle at 40 paces!

(Bet you can't guess who's most scared of the dentist. Jade? Uh-uh – she's way too chilled. Cloe? She actually loves the dentist! Yasmin? Pretty Princess is super-cool about getting her teeth checked. Yep, it's Bunny Boo who's the chicken – although it's just about the only thing she is scared of!)

Beauty SOS!

Dab a little toothpaste on the spot before you go to sleep.

MUSICAL MAESTRO

ACOUSTIC GUITAR

How does it work?
You play the acoustic guitar by plucking, strumming or slapping the strings over a hole in the hollow body. The sound is rich and vibrant.

How easy is it?
You can start making music really quickly, but expect sore fingertips at first! This is a great instrument to start off with.

Where have I heard it?
Classical, Spanish and folk music use the acoustic guitar a lot – but the best thing is that it is so easy to carry around. So you will have heard street buskers, friends and local bands playing it too! Check out James Blunt's music for some mellow acoustic guitar melodies!

ELECTRIC GUITAR

How does it work?
The electric guitar turns the vibrations of the strings into electrical currents. The signal is fed into an amplifier to produce the final sound.

How easy is it?
The electric guitar is heavier and slightly more complex than the acoustic guitar, so start off with the acoustic and move on to the electric afterwards.

Where have I heard it?
This instrument is super-versatile and you can hear it in rock 'n' roll, metal, country, pop, jazz and blues. Check out Avril Lavigne and the Arctic Monkeys!

VIOLIN

How does it work?
The violin is a small instrument that has four strings. It is tucked under the chin and played with a bow. When the bow is moved across the strings, it vibrates them, making a magical sound. It can seem almost like a voice sometimes!

How easy is it?
It takes a bit of practice, because this is an ultra-delicate instrument! While you are learning, you are gonna make some stupendous screeching sounds … but when you can play haunting melodies and make beautiful sounds, it will all have been worth it.

Where have I heard it?
Classical, folk and Celtic music often uses the violin. Scope out The Corrs to hear how violins can sound fresh and totally hot!

PIANO

How does it work?
The piano works by striking steel strings with felt hammers. The vibrations of the strings make the sound.

How easy is it?
Being able to play the piano is an awesome skill for anyone who's interested in music. It'll be a major help whether you are writing songs, singing or playing. It takes good coordination because you need to move your fingers and hands in different ways at the same time.

Where have I heard it?
The piano is used in tons of music styles – from old-style classical to modern R&B. Check out the Scissor Sisters or Jamie Cullum!

Have you ever wished you could play a musical instrument? If you want to learn, then go for it! Seize your chance and make all your dreams come true. Here's our take on some of the hottest instruments out there!

HARP

This super-cool instrument has lasted for hundreds of years – it was even played in Ancient Egypt! Queen Marie Antoinette of France played it, so if you feel like following in the steps of a real-life queen, this is the instrument for you!

How does it work?
The harp is a string instrument, so you pluck the string to make the sound, just like a guitar. It sounds totally romantic and magical!

How easy is it?
Like all musical instruments, it takes practice to sound great. You will use all your fingers apart from your little fingers. Some harps have pedals, so you might use your feet as well. It takes patience and coordination to become a harpist!

Where have I heard it?
The harp is used in most classical music, often for special effects. There are some harpists in pop music too – check out some of Björk's songs.

DRUM

The drum can make a completely massive sound! It comes in all shapes and sizes, but all drums have a sort of 'skin' that is stretched over a frame. The drum can be played with your hand or a stick.

How does it work?
The drum is hit with a huge beater but can sometimes be played using the hand or fingers for special effect.

How easy is it?
Start with a smaller drum – it is difficult at first, but keep going. A drum machine or a practice pad is a good way to start – and a lil' bit quieter too, until you get the hang of it!

Where have I heard it?
Drums are really important in most modern music. Check out Harry from McFly or the awesome drummer from Snow Patrol!

TRUMPET

The trumpet is made from a brass tube, which is bent into shape. It makes a very loud, strong sound, which can be heard high above the rest of the band!

How does it work?
To play the trumpet you have to vibrate your lips over the mouthpiece. There are three valves on top of the trumpet. When they are pressed, they produce different notes.

How easy is it?
This is a kinda easy instrument to learn, so give it a try!

Where have I heard it?
Listen to trumpet legends Miles Davis or Louis Armstrong for some totally awesome inspiration!

SAXOPHONE

How does it work?
The awesome sax sound is made by blowing across a reed while fingering the keys that cover the holes along the length of the sax.

How easy is it?
If you ever played the recorder, you'll find it easy to learn the sax – your fingers have to move in the same way.

It's gonna feel weird at first because you have to use your diaphragm to play, and it's a heavy instrument to carry. But the sound is as smooth as silk!

Where have I heard it?
John Coltrane and Courtney Pine are super-famous sax players – raid your 'rents music collection for some old-style sounds!

© MGA

WORD CHALLENGE

**Sasha loves puzzles – they're like workouts for your brain!
How many words can you make from this phrase?**

"SASHA IS A MEGA MUSIC DIVA!"

_____
_____
_____
_____
_____
_____
_____
_____
_____
_____
_____
_____
_____
_____
_____
_____
_____
_____

ROCKIN' STYLIST

We love stepping up in front of the camera and belting out our fave tunes to make stunning music videos. But you can never be seen on screen in the same outfit twice! Design an outfit for Pretty Princess to wear in our next music video. It's a rockin' song so make sure you create a look that's totally dazzling!

© MGA

Video Vogue

Part 1

"I can't believe
how much homework
I've had this week!"
exclaimed Sasha.
She dropped a pile of essays and
projects onto her desk in the media
studies classroom and collapsed into her
chair with a huge sigh. Her friends nodded
in sympathy.
"I know!" said Cloe, who was already in her
seat. "There were tons of things I wanted to
do after school this week, and I couldn't do any
of them! I've had a major geography
assignment and a really complicated maths test
to revise for and a-"
"We've all had them, remember?" said Jade with
a grin. She leaned over to Cloe. **"Chill out,
drama mama. It's Friday, it's the last lesson
of the day and all our homework
assignments are done. Nothing is gonna
stop me from hitting the mall
this weekend!"**
Cloe returned her grin, thinking
about all the fashion-forward
clothes she wanted to
locate at the mall.

"Good afternoon, everyone!" said a loud voice.

Mr Lee, their media studies teacher, strode into the room. Yasmin was right behind him, and she slid into her seat beside Jade as Mr Lee walked to the front of the classroom. Jade, Sasha and Cloe looked at her in surprise. It was very unlike Yasmin to be late for a class.

"Cutting it fine, girlfriend," said Jade.

"I know!" panted Yasmin. "But I had to finish typing up my creative writing assignment and then I had to run over to the English classroom to hand in my essay."

She started pulling out her books and pens, still trying to catch her breath.

"I think all our teachers have gone crazy this week," said Cloe. **"It's the only possible explanation!"**

"At least this lesson should be laid back," said Sasha. "Media studies is always fun!"

©MGA

While Mr Lee was opening his briefcase, Jade leaned towards her friends. "We have worked way too hard this week," she whispered. **"Are you guys pumped for a lil' retail relaxation over the weekend?"**

"You know it!" said Yasmin, happily.

"So cool!" added Cloe and Sasha. At that moment, Mr Lee looked up at the class and cleared his throat. Everyone went quiet.

"I have some good news," he said.

"You will be excited to know that we are not going to have a lesson this afternoon."

There was a loud roar of cheers and whoops.

"I really like Mr Lee!" said Cloe.

"Thank goodness he hasn't got the 'huge amounts of homework' bug that the other teachers seem to have caught!" added Sasha.

"A weekend of shopping, here we come," said Jade.

All the other students were having similar conversations. Mr Lee laughed and held up his hand.

"Settle down, settle down," he said. "I have a really exciting assignment for you, and I want you to start right away. You can get into groups and stay here if you like, or you can head over to the library, or wherever you feel like working."

"Hmmm," said Sasha. **"Maybe I spoke too soon."**

"Working in the media is often about hitting really tight deadlines," Mr Lee went on.

"I don't like the sound of this," Yasmin whispered.

"So you are going to see how you cope under pressure," he said. **"By first thing Monday morning, I want to see a piece of original film from each group. I want to see you using imagination and vision. You've got two and a half days to come up with something that will amaze me!"**

Yasmin, Cloe, Jade and Sasha looked at each other and groaned.

"There goes our trip to the mall," said Jade, running her fingers through her silky dark hair.

"There goes our relaxation time," added Cloe. "I've changed my mind - I don't like Mr Lee at all!"

"Let's face it, girls," said Sasha. "There goes our entire weekend!"

"Not necessarily," said Yasmin slowly. The other three turned to her in surprise. There was a sudden sparkle in her eyes as she looked at them.

"What do you mean, Pretty Princess?" asked Cloe, sensing that her friend had an idea.

"Well, it depends what sort of video we make, doesn't it?" said Yasmin, putting her hand on her hip. **"Listen, we have been planning to do something to promote our rock band for ages, right?"**

©MGA

"Right!" said the other three. "And we've really struggled to find the time for any practice this week, because of all the homework, right?"

"Right!" said the others again.

"So let's make a music video!" said Yasmin. "We already have a ton of awesome songs to choose from, plus the instruments and the video stars!"

"Meaning us!" said Cloe, clapping her hands together.

"That means the only things we have to find are a venue and some super-hot outfits!" said Yasmin in triumph.

"And that means a trip to the mall, which is music to my ears!" Jade said with a laugh.

"This way we can spend time together, promote the Rock Angelz and complete our assignment!" Yasmin said. "What do you think?"

"I think that this is only to be an awesome weekend after all!" said Cloe, hugging her.

"It's a totally, completely and utterly slammin' idea!" said Sasha, hugging Yasmin. **"We can have so much fun with this! But we've got to get organised."**
"And those words are music to your ears, Bunny Boo," said Jade.
The girls all laughed. Sasha was definitely cut out to be a leader - she loved nothing better than making plans and getting organised!
"Jade, will you hit the shops and pick out some super-stylin' looks for us all?" asked Sasha. "You've got the best eye for the latest and greatest looks - just make sure it's gonna fit with our vibe."
"I'm on it," said Jade, picking up her bag and heading for the mall.
"Jade's got such a knack for spotting the hottest trends," said Yasmin. "I just know she's gonna find some awesome outfits for us!"

"Cloe," continued Sasha, "can you locate a venue - something that's gonna look scorchin' as a truly artistic backdrop to our music?"

"No problem," said Cloe. She grabbed her car keys and whisked out of the door, her long, blonde hair flying out behind her.

Cloe was super-artistic and she always found stunning locations for their Bratz magazine photo shoots. Sasha felt sure that she would snag an eye-poppin' venue.

"What about me?" asked Yasmin.

"We're gonna need a truly roof-raisin' number for this video," said Sasha. "Can you go through our songs and pick out one for us to perform? You need to make sure that all our guitars and sound equipment are ready too."

"Consider it done," said Yasmin with a smile. "I can't wait to get started! I'll tune all the guitars up and test the equipment."

"What about you, Bunny Boo?"

"We need someone to work the camera when we're all performing," said Sasha. "I'm gonna call in a favour!"

©MGA

37

A few hours later, Cloe, Yasmin and Sasha each received a text message from Jade:

CU at my pad for stylin' session!

They knew exactly what that meant - Jade had put together four outfits for the video! They all rushed to her house as fast as they could. They sat down on the soft beanbags in Jade's room and she served them with fruity smoothies. Then she went to stand in front of the wardrobe.
"I went for an ultra-modern style with a retro vibe," she said. "The first outfit is for Cloe."
She pulled the first outfit from the wardrobe and the girls gasped in delight. Jade had picked out a black silk mini with a denim trim, teamed with a scoop-neck black tee and a powder-blue skinny scarf.

38

There were gold beads to wrap around Cloe's neck and waist. Knee-length white boots with a gold trim completed the look. "I love it!" squealed Cloe, hugging Jade. **"It's just like having a real stylist! This look is absolutely perfect, Kool Kat!"**

"Next up is Sasha," said Jade, pulling out the second outfit.

Sasha's image mixed ultra glam with rockin' cool - a jersey lilac dress combined with a matching faux-fur bolero. With a red chain-link necklace and cream cowboy boots, the outfit had Sasha's name written all over it. **"This is tight!"** said Sasha, pressing the outfit against her and checking out her reflection in the mirror. "Good job, Kool Kat!"

"Now it's Yasmin's turn," said Jade, revealing the third outfit.

Yasmin's look was super-cool and stylin', with indigo skinny jeans and a pale blue tee. Faux-fur-lined blue boots and a white skinny scarf gave the ensemble a truly regal quality.

©MGA

39

It was finished off with a purple fedora hat that was the essence of cool.

"**Dazzlin'!**" Yasmin said, her eyes dancing with excitement. "I can't wait to try it on!"

"**And ... last but not least ...**" said Jade.

She held up her own outfit - a heavenly purple mini with a matching long-sleeved top and a groovin' cream-coloured waistcoat. With long, cream boots and a string of cream beads, it was classy and funky.

"That purple shade will totally accentuate your eyes," said Cleo. "I've got the perfect eyeshadow to go with it!"

"**You did an amazing job finding these fabulous outfits,**" said Sasha.

"It was one of the easiest shopping trips ever!" Jade admitted modestly. "All the pieces and accessories just jumped out at me. Do you really think they work?"

"They could have been made for us," said Yasmin. "Each outfit looks awesome on its own…"

"But together they're outta this world!" Sasha finished.

©MGA

"I've picked out a song that's gonna team up perfectly with these looks," said Yasmin. **"'On the Edge'** - it's one of my faves."

"Oh, mine too!" gasped Jade. "That's so weird - I was even humming that song when I was picking out these fashions!"

"Great choice, Pretty Princess," said Sasha.

"All the instruments and equipment are ready too," said Yasmin. "I also printed out copies of the lyrics - it's quite a long time since we sang it on stage!"

"Good call, Pretty Princess," said Jade. "How about the cameras, Sasha - have you found someone to film us?"

"I've asked Meygan to help us with the filming, and she's gonna hook up with us at the venue," said Sasha.

"Great," said Yasmin. **"Meygan's got a sharp eye for a good shot!"**

"How's your hunt for the venue coming along, Angel?" Sasha asked Cloe.

Cloe sank down on the end of Jade's bed.

"Awful," she cried. **"I don't know what to do!** I drove around town all afternoon after school, checking out locations. But there was just nowhere that would work for a music video!"

The other three girls looked at her in concern.

"But if we don't have a background setting, we can't make the film," said Sasha.

"I know!" Cloe wailed. "You guys have all done so well, and I'm the only one holding us up! I'm gonna go out first thing in the morning and drive over to Uptown City. There's bound to be something there, right?"

"Sure," said Yasmin, putting her arm around Cloe. "Don't worry, Angel - you'll find the perfect place, I know it."

©MGA

"Totally," said Jade. **"You can do anything, Angel!"** "We all believe in you," said Sasha, and they shared a group hug.

The girls spent the rest of the evening working out a storyboard plan for their video. They had to know exactly what shots they needed and where the cameras needed to stand. It was super-important to decide how they were going to shoot the song - who was going to have a close up, when they would focus in on the guitars and when they would do long shots of all four of them together. It was late when they had finally agreed on a plan. Yasmin gave a wide yawn.

"I need to go to bed," she said. **"This is great fun - but it's super-tiring too!"** "Ditto," said Jade. "We're gonna be on camera tomorrow, girls, so let's get our beauty sleep!"

©MGA

Makeup Mistress

The perfect makeup look works with your outfit, your colouring and the venue. But you've gotta think about more than that when you're picking out a look.

You should wear totally different makeup during the day than in the evening. For daytime, keep your look fresh and simple. In the evening, you can use a few darker, richer shades.

Use these faces to design two rockin' new makeup styles!

A Puzzling Time!

Check out this Kakuro puzzle. Can you solve it?

• There are numbers in the gold squares. These numbers are called clues.

• Each square is divided by a diagonal slash. The number in the top right corner is an 'across' clue. The number in the bottom left corner is a 'down' clue.

• You must insert numbers from 1 to 9 into the white squares to add up to the clue.

• You can't repeat any number twice in the same entry.

Hint: Start off with the '4' and '17' clues!

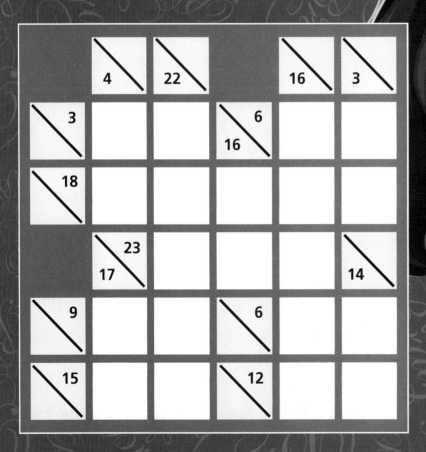

©MGA

The Writing

I've definitely got the writing bug, and I scribble down ideas all the time. But it takes real dedication to pull those ideas together and write a story. Check out some of my hottest tips and then get writing. This could be the start of something big, girl! One day you could be a famous author, or even watching your story being turned into a film!

Preparation

• Find a quiet place where you can write with no interruptions.

• If you're working on computer, make sure that your desk is clear except for the keyboard, mouse and screen.

• If you're writing old-style, choose a fabulously funky notebook and a smooth pen.

• Make sure you've got some snacks and refreshing drinks handy - writing is hard work and you are gonna get hungry!

Plot

• Stick a sheet of A3 paper on the wall and draw vertical and horizontal lines to make a grid, kinda like a comic strip!

• In each square, write one important thing that's gonna happen in your story. You might need more sheets of paper - that's okay!

• When you've finished, you'll have a plan of the whole plot of your story. Check it out. Look for places where the plot is weak, or where it gets super-complicated. This will help you to have a clear idea of what you're gonna write.

• Just because you've got a plan, doesn't mean you have to stick to it! But it gives you a starting place for your writing.

Characters

• You need to know your characters inside out! You need to know how they are going to react to any situation. So take some time to think about each one of them. Which ones do you like? Which characters irritate you? Which seem the most alive in your imagination?

• Create a background story for each character. It doesn't matter if that never gets into your story! Just so long as you know where they were born, where they went to school and any important events in their life.

• Names are powerful things! Pick up some name books from car boot sales or markets - they'll be a great inspiration. Use the sound of a name to tell the reader something about the character.

Bug

Point of view

• Who is going to be telling the story? Whose point of view is the reader going to be hearing? There are three main choices.

• First person - This means that you write as if the story happened to you. You can only tell the reader what you are thinking and feeling.

• Third person limited - You describe the story happening to someone else, but it's as if you can only see through that character's eyes. You don't know what any other character is thinking or feeling, and you can only go where that character goes.

• Third person omniscient - As the writer, you know everything! You describe the story and the characters as if you are describing a film you watched - you can tell the reader what all the characters are thinking and feeling, and you can jump from scene to scene as often as you like.

Cliffhangers

• Think about your fave TV soap. Something exciting always happens right at the end of the episode, right? You have to tune in next time to find out what happens next. That's a cliffhanger! It's as if you are leaving your main character hanging from the edge of a cliff. You have to find out if they're gonna fall!

• Books have cliffhangers too - usually at the end of a chapter. Make a list of the most exciting moments in your story. How many do you have?

• Now you can plan where your chapters will fall. They don't all have to end with a cliffhanger - too many is overkill! But planning them before you start writing will help give your story energy.

Dialogue

• Dialogue is the conversation that your characters have. It's gotta sound real! Listen to the conversations your friends have. Copy some of them down, or record them. This will give you a great start and help you to write dialogue that sounds real.

• When people talk in real life, they say things like 'um' and 'er' all the time. That would be super-boring to read, so you can cut that out. It doesn't need to be that realistic!

• If you listen to your friends talking, you'll find out that they each have certain words or phrases that they use a lot. You can use that when you are writing words for your characters to speak. Give them accents, words or phrases that only belong to them!

©MGA

Make your

Funky, personalised scrapbooks are the latest trend and we all love making them! Check out our step-by-step guide to making your own unique book!

1

What's your passion? Give your scrapbooks a theme or a purpose. Yasmin's scrapbook is full of the coolest ideas for stories. She gets inspiration from all sorts of places - newspaper cuttings, photos, even conversations she overhears in the street! Cloe packs her scrapbook with colours, textures and patterns that she can use in her art

2

Size doesn't matter! It totally depends on how you want to use your scrapbook. A big book is great if you're going to keep it at home - but if you want to carry it with you, choose a small book that will fit into your handbag.

3

Grab your paints, felt tips or colouring pencils, and design a first page that really stands out! You could write your name and date of birth on there, or draw a picture of yourself. You could give your scrapbook a title, or list the things you're gonna collect in it.

4

Without borders, some of your pages could end up looking really bare. Practise drawing some far-out and funky borders for the pages of your book. Here's one to get you started! Use a pencil to draw the outline of the border first. Then add colour and glitter! You could draw a different border on each page, or alternate two all the way through.

own scrapbook

5 If you're gonna have the best scrapbook ever, it's gotta be bursting with interesting things! So start collecting right now. Choose a box or a folder where you can keep your fabulous finds until you're ready to put them into your scrapbook. You can put anything in there! Postcards, recipes, flowers, menus, tickets, fave words - there are no rules and no limits!

6 You can use anything to put your finds into your book. You might need glue, a stapler, colourful paperclips or sticky tape. Keep them in the same box with your finds so that you are always ready to go!

7 Keep your eyes out for super-cool pens in bright colours. If the pages of your book are dark, try using silver and gold pens to write your notes. Your pages should be jam-packed with pictures, cuttings, samples and notes. Don't worry about having to turn the page sideways to fit in your notes, or using different coloured pens. It just makes your book more interesting and exciting!

8 If your BFFs love scrapbooks too, start a scrapbook club! You could put anything you don't need for your scrapbook into a central box that anyone can use. Meet once a week to show each other how your books have developed and to share ideas!

©MGA

Crossword

Across

1. A city with a leaning tower.
3. A sport that's played with long, curved sticks.
5. A game that involves hearts and queens.
7. Last.
9. One of the Tweevils.
10. Giving someone a whole new look.
11. The editor of Your Thing Magazine.

Down

1. A high and stylin' type of shoe.
2. A place to get your facial and manicure.
3. The home of the movies.
4. An Australian animal.
6. Someone who helps you when you're ill.
8. A style that uses past fashions.

Nail Natural

Cloe loves dreaming up new ideas for fabulous nail art - and trying them out on her friends' nails! Use these pictures to design your own nail designs. Check the colours of nail varnish you have, and make sure you have clean, tiny brushes. Treat the nails like mini canvases and create miniature works of art!

©MGA

20 Routes to a Rockin' Bedroom!

1 Ask your 'rents if you can pick a brand-new colour scheme for your room, starting with the walls. Whether you go for paint or paper, make sure it's stylin', girlfriend!

2 Check out all the handles that are in your room - on your door, desk, wardrobe and drawers. Are they looking old and boring? Head to your nearest hardware shop and buy some funky new ones that'll change the whole look of your room!

3 Cushions can add colour and chic to your room, arranged on your bed or on a chair.

4 There are tons of brightly coloured, vibrant throws out there right now, and they will give your bedroom an immediate facelift. Choose cool citrus colours for a fresh, summery look, or rich jewel shades for winter warmth!

5 If your 'rents agree, you can use a new carpet to totally change the look of your room. Lighter colours will make your room seem larger, and deeper colours will add a touch of high drama.

6 Pick out some stylin' storage boxes to help declutter your boudoir. Think clean and crisp - putting clutter out of sight will make your room look bigger and more welcoming. Check out rolling boxes that will slide under your bed, and oval white boxes will look stunning on top of your wardrobe.

7 The more gorgeous your desk is, the more time you'll want to spend at it! Make it a happenin' place to do your homework. If it's made of wood, sand it down and varnish it to make it gleam. Otherwise, try repainting in a rich new colour, or draw stencil pics onto the drawers. Have fun with it!

8 Burn joss sticks or scented oils to make your room fragrant. (Be sure to check with your 'rents first, though!)

9 Put your fave snaps into polished silver photo frames and stand them in groups of three or four.

10 Choose some sumptuous curtains and attach tiebacks to the wall for a truly glam look!

Are you tired of your room?

Have you had the same uninspiring shades for way too long?

Here's your chance to change all that!

©MGA

11 Brighten up old wardrobes and chests of drawers by painting them gleaming white. Use pewter knobs to create a scorchin' retro look.

12 If you can't get a new carpet, cover the old one with thick, luxurious rugs in jewel colours.

13 Choose pictures for your walls that really mean something to you. Then pick gorgeous frames for them and make a slammin' artistic statement! Be bold and daring - choose a giant picture for one wall, or frame a totally stunning piece of fabric to create a focal point.

14 Think about the layout of your room. Has your bed always been in the same position? Move it! Changing the position of your furniture can make your room feel totally different.

15 Collect some stylish vases and always have freshly cut flowers in your room.

16 Throw away that dullsville old lampshade and replace it with something fashion-forward and funky. Use table lamps or standing lamps to create a more ambient vibe.

17 Hang a mini pin-board above your desk for postcards, notes, reminders and your jammin' social calendar!

18 Make your bedroom a traveller's paradise. Display the ornaments and fabrics you have bought when you've been on holiday. Think of masks from Venice, shawls from Spain or parasols from China!

19 Whittle down your wardrobe. Take out any outfits that you don't wear, any old shoes, coats, belts or accessories. Then persuade your 'rents to do a car boot sale - you'll make enough to buy some brand-new outfits!

20 Line your drawers with scented paper so your clothes always smell divine.

Jade's Fashion Tips

Check it out - I always have the inside scope on what's hot and what's not this season. Take a trip down the catwalk with the most scorchin' looks of the century!

Ask Yourself

What's my style?
Are you the girl next door or the slammin' rock chick? You've gotta feel comfortable in what you wear, so make fashions fit your style, not the other way around!

What's my colour?
Stand in front of a mirror and hold up some colours to your face. What washes you out? What makes you glow?

Shhh!

Cotton is gonna make a big comeback, so make sure you pick up some bargains before everyone finds out! Think smocked blouses and gypsy chic.

Dress to Impress

Dresses are still big news for the new season, so think feminine and floaty!

Dark Colours

The hottest darker shades are gonna be rich and vibrant tones of purple, red and green. Trust me on this, girlfriend!

Pale Colours

Think sweet pastels in pink, blue and yellow, and create a soft, gentle vibe that everyone will flock to copy!

Watch Out!

When you're accessorising this season, put your watch at the top of your list. There are some fabulous fashion watches out there at fantastic prices. Buy a new watch instead of a new handbag, and you'll definitely be 'ahead of your time'!

Top Textures

When you're picking out fabrics, think about the feel of them as well as the colour. They shouldn't be completely plain - go for super-shiny or metallic styles that will get you noticed!

Moods

The fashion moods that are gonna go big are romantic and luxurious, with an edgy, modern twist. Natural beauty, the great outdoors and golden glows are all heading your way!

Catwalk Characters

**Each new style has a character - which one works best for you?
Can you guess which one is my fave?**

Sorceress

The Sorceress is a mistress of disguise! She chooses dark, rich fabrics and warm jewellery in gold and bronze. She seems to shine, and her opulent clothes are cut in simple, clean lines that reflect her beauty.

Goddess

The goddess is confident, dramatic and romantic. Wherever she goes, she commands attention! Her clothes are extravagant and intricate, with a simple, classic design at the core. White and blue are her fave shades, and diamonds are her fave jewels!

Gypsy

The gypsy loves the freedom and beauty of nature, and it shows in floating fabrics, bright colours and jingling accessories. There are no hard lines in this girl's style, and her vibe is warm and musical!

Super-heroine

The super-heroine has a sharp wit and an even sharper style. She's always cool, calm and collected, and she wears crisp colours with a sculptured, tailored edge. Black, red and pink are her signature colours.

P.S.
Check out Cloe's matching makeup tips on page 104!

Jade x

55

Hollywood Hot Spot

"We're never gonna make the deadline," said Cloe, burying her head in her hands. "We're gonna miss our printer's schedule and the magazine won't come out and we'll have to finish *Bratz* magazine and-"

"Angel, it'll be okay," said Yasmin gently. "If we all work together I know that we can get it done. I just have to finish off my article, and you need to complete the design of one more spread."

"But what about Jade's fashion shoot?" wailed Cloe. "We still have to do that, check the pictures, create the magazine pages and write the captions. But the model we had lined up can't make it, the venue has cancelled and the deadline's tomorrow!"

Yasmin rubbed her friend's arm sympathetically. Cloe was definitely having one of her drama-mama days.

"She has a point," said Sasha. "How are we going to do that fashion shoot with no model and no venue?"

Yasmin looked at her in surprise. Sasha was usually the first to get annoyed with Cloe for freaking out.

"Hey, it's not like you to accept defeat, Bunny Boo!" said Yasmin. "Jade can be our model for the shoot - she totally knows how to work the hottest new styles, right? And as for a venue, who needs one? The best designers get their inspiration from the street, so that's where we'll do the shoot - on the hip and happenin' streets of Stilesville!"

Before Sasha could reply, there was a squeal from Clo's desk.

"That's a great idea, Pretty Princess!" she cried, sitting up and smiling. "Give me ten minutes and I will finish this final spread - then we can get out there with the camera!"

©MGA

At that moment,
the door of their studio
opened and Jade walked in,
looking really depressed.
"What's the matter. Kool Kat?" asked
Yasmin, rushing to her side.
Jade blinked her big green eyes sadly and
looked at Yasmin.
"Guess who's in town?" she said.
"A top fashion designer?" Yasmin guessed.
"A world-famous hip-hop band?" said
Sasha hopefully.
"No," sighed Jade. **"It's Jay Oz."**
The others gasped.
"Jay Oz - as in the super-famous, totally
awesome Hollywood director?" Sasha
shrieked. "I love his movies!"
"Exactly," said Jade. "He's shooting a couple
of extra scenes for his new movie right here in
Stilesville - and he wants local people to be
background extras."
Yasmin gaped at her and Sasha started fanning
herself with a copy of Bratz magazine.
"Omigosh!" Cloe squealed. "This is
amazing! This is a dream come true!
When are the auditions? We've
gotta go, right, you guys?"

"That's the problem," said Jade, sinking into her chair and staring at all the work that she had to do. "The film's almost finished and these are really late, last-minute extra scenes. Auditions are happening right now. There's no way we can go! The magazine has to be finished by midday tomorrow."

"And we can't let our readers down," groaned Sasha. "This is terrible!" The girls stared at each other in horror. The biggest chance ever to star in a real Hollywood movie - and there was no way they could do it!

"Don't be blue," said Yasmin after a long silence. "We'll get another chance someday. But right now we have to get that fashion shoot started!"

"Pretty Princess is right," said Sasha firmly. "Our readers are super-loyal and there is no way we're gonna let them down."

"You know it!" said Jade.

"Cool!" they all shouted, giving a big high-five.

Soon, the four girls were out on the streets of Stilesville, hunting down awesome locations to really show off the fashions. They always did this at the last minute to keep them edgy and fresh.

Each month they showcased the latest talent, and this month it was a glam new line from a budding young designer. They had all been looking forward to the photo shoot, and they made up their minds to forget all about the auditions.

"These gowns are so off the hook," said Jade as she posed in front of a billboard.

"You look spectacular!" said Sasha as she snapped the pictures. Cloe darted in to freshen up Jade's makeup and Yasmin adjusted the lighting.

"I can't wait to tell our readers all about these designs," said Yasmin. "I keep thinking up captions while I'm watching the shoot - I hope I can remember them all!"

"Okay, I've got enough shots here," said Sasha eventually. "Jade, can you put on that stylin' silver dress - I don't have any shots of that yet."

"I think this would look fabulous against these high stone walls and railings over here," said Jade. **"I love the contrast of the glitz and the street!"**

The girls moved their gear and set up the lights again. Cloe checked Jade's makeup and handed her some accessories.

They were so focused on the shoot that they didn't notice a small group of people watching them nearby. One of the men was pointing at them and waving his arms around excitedly. He was young and handsome, and dressed in a totally individual style. The people around him were shrugging and shaking their heads, and he seemed to be arguing with them.

61

Oblivious to the drama nearby, Jade moved and posed in the dress as Sasha walked around her, taking as many pictures as she could. The afternoon sped by as they worked on finishing the shoot before the light faded.

"That's it!" Sasha called out eventually. **"Jade, that dress is sizzlin' - it could have been made for you!"**

"Made for you to wear on the red carpet," added Cloe, giving Jade a hug.

"That would be a dream come true!" said Jade with a laugh.

"Maybe I can help you with that," said a voice.

The girls turned around and saw the man who had been watching them earlier. Yasmin didn't recognise him, but Sasha gasped.

"It's Jay Oz!" she said.

The handsome young director was grinning at them.

"Call me Jay," he said. "I've been watching you four girls. It's plain to see that you are great friends - you work really well together as a team."

©MGA

62

"Thanks," said Jade with a laid-back smile. "We're from Bratz magazine - we're finishing off a fashion shoot for a super-tight deadline."

"Then I won't hold you up," smiled Jay. "But I'm hoping that you might be able to help me out tomorrow afternoon. We've been auditioning for extras all day, but I'm still short of four girls. I need people who are going to come across as great friends. **Do you think you might be able to help me out?**"

All four girls were staring at him with their mouths open. Sasha was the first one to find her voice.

"We would totally, absolutely, definitely love to!" she said.

"Then I'll see you right here at one o'clock tomorrow," he said.

He waved at them and walked away. The girls looked at each other.

"That is …" said Jade.

"… so completely …" added Yasmin.

"… unbelievably …" said Cloe.

"COOL!" they yelled together.

©MGA

Next morning,
Jade, Sasha, Cloe and
Yasmin arrived early at the
studio. The four friends started to
do what they did best - working as a
team. Sasha picked out the best shots
from the shoot and Jade dropped them
onto the pages she had designed.
**"You look dazzlin' in these shots, Kool
Kat,"** Sasha said. "Because you know the
fashions so well, you model them better than
anyone else could!"
"Thanks," laughed Jade, "but don't start getting
ideas, Bunny Boo. I'm not doing the modelling
every month!"
Cleo created some tiny swirls and diamond shapes
to place in between the pictures, and Yasmin
wrote sizzlin' captions that described the outfits
and told readers where to buy them.
"This is going to be the best issue yet,"
said Jade, checking over the pages as they
were completed.
"You always say that!" called out her
friends in unison.
"But it's always true!"
Jade giggled.

©MGA

At last the final pictures and words had been added, and they checked the whole magazine to make sure everything looked fabulous. Then they burnt the magazine to disc and couriered it over to the printers.

"We did it!" said Jade with relief. "Just in time!"

"Speaking of time, it's quarter to one!" Cloe exclaimed, looking at her watch. "Come on - we've gotta run!"

"You know it, girl," laughed Jade as she grabbed her bag. **"All the way to Hollywood!"**

"No, I mean really run!" said Cloe. "I haven't got my car here today!"

The girls hurried out of the door and raced across town as fast as they could.

"I wonder what we'll be filming," panted Yasmin.

"Hopefully not something where we have to run!" puffed Sasha. "I'm work out already!"

"We have already done a day's work," said Jade.

"I love days like this, though," Cloe added. **"Packed with excitement!"**

©MGA

When they arrived at the filming location, Jay Oz waved at them eagerly.

"Great to see you!" he said. "We've got some great outfits for you to wear - we want you all to look glamorous for this scene!"

"No complaints from us!" said Jade. The girls were dressed by the wardrobe mistress. Each of them was given a pair of slim-leg trousers and a shimmering top. They posed in front of the mirrors, checking out their new images.

"These are super-stylin'," said Jade. "I would love to work on the wardrobe for a film one day!"

"It's great fun," said the wardrobe mistress. "But today you're going to be in front of the camera! Have you seen your scripts?"

The friends checked the scripts.

"Omigosh!" said Cloe. "We actually get to say a few lines each!"

"The main thing I want to see is that great chemistry you guys have," Jay said. **"I want to see you all sparkle!"**

©MGA

The film crew and cast worked hard all afternoon. The four friends soon finished their parts, but Jay invited them to hang around and watch the rest of the filming.

At the end of the day, Jay took them to their fave mall café and treated them to fruit smoothies.

"You girls were great," he said. "I didn't think I was ever going to find four people who were believable as friends - and then I saw you working together on that fashion shoot!"

"Thank you so much for the chance to be film stars!" said Cloe, sipping her smoothie. "We thought that we had no chance of auditioning because we had to finish the magazine on time."

"Seeing you working together on the fashion shoot was better than any audition," said Jay. "I'd like to invite you all to the premiere of the movie next month. Will you come?"

The girls squealed and hugged each other.

"Just try to stop us!" laughed Yasmin.

©MGA

BRATZ
™

One month later, Jay Oz walked down the red carpet towards the cinema where his movie was premiering. The stars of the film were busy signing autographs, but next to him were four beautiful girls in stunning gowns. The crowd was a mass of flashing lights as people photographed the mystery girls. Everyone was buzzing with the question - who were they?

Although they looked super-cool, the four friends could hardly believe that they were actually on the red carpet with Jay Oz!

"I love these stunning gowns!" said Yasmin, who was in a gold, shimmering dress.

"I love the crowds and the vibe!" said Sasha, waving at the photographers. She was wearing a pale-blue dress that swept the floor.

68

BRATZ™

"I love meeting all the stars!" said Cloe, whose black gown shone with sequins.

"I love movies!" cried Jade, spinning around in delight in her silvery dress. **"This really is a dream come true!"**

More cameras flashed and photographers and journalists shouted out questions to them.

"Our dresses are sparkling under all the electric lights!" Yasmin laughed.

"What really sparkles in your onscreen chemistry," said Jay. "It's extras like you girls who help make a film truly great!"

The girls linked arms and smiled at Jay.

"Thanks," said Sasha. "But I think our off-screen friendship is the thing that sparkles most of all!"

"You know it!" said her friends.

©MGA

Movie Mad!

How many times a month do you head to the cinema with your friends? If you're movie mad like us, you've probably seen dozens of films and picked up on what a makes a rockin' film. Here's your chance to be a film director!

1. Imagine that you're making a film with your friends. It could be an action movie, a scary film or even a romantic comedy!

2. Think up a scene from the film. Think about what's going to happen in the scene and whose faces you want to see.

3. Use this storyboard to plan out each shot that you're gonna take with the camera. Remember, you've only got 19 shots, so think carefully.

4. Start by drawing out the scenes in pencil. When you're happy with all the shots, go over the lines with a black pen and write the scene instructions under the picture.

5. Go, girl! You just planned out your first film scene! Next stop, Hollywood …

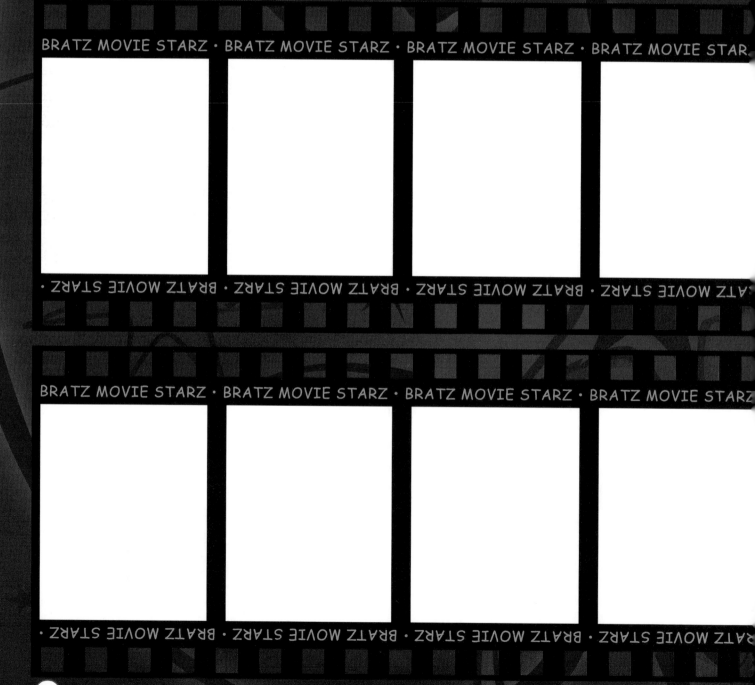

BRATZ MOVIE STARZ • BRATZ MOVIE STARZ • BRATZ MOVIE STARZ • BRATZ MOVIE STARZ

BRATZ MOVIE STARZ • BRATZ MOVIE STARZ • BRATZ MOVIE STARZ • BRATZ MOVIE STARZ •

BRATZ MOVIE STARZ • BRATZ MOVIE STARZ • BRATZ MOVIE STARZ • BRATZ MOVIE STARZ

BRATZ MOVIE STARZ • BRATZ MOVIE STARZ • BRATZ MOVIE STARZ • BR

BRATZ MOVIE STARZ • BRATZ MOVIE STARZ • BRATZ MOVIE STARZ

Movie

What kind of films would you act in if you were a movie star?

1. You're in the middle of the mall when a really cute guy starts singing a song you know. He's looking right at you - what do you do?

a. Listen to his gorgeous voice as he serenades you, and then wait for him to make his next move. This must be true love! ✓

b. Run away! Run away! ☐

c. Join in at the top of your voice - this guy is obviously all about living in the moment, just like you! ☐

d. There's something super-weird about this. You scope out the area, searching for clues to what's really going on here! ☐

2. You're in a dark wood at midnight when you see a wooden hut up ahead. What do you think is inside?

a. Your boyfriend, with a candlelit romantic meal, a book of poetry and a huge bunch of flowers. ☐

b. Nothing - it will be empty and deserted. You believe in being realistic. ✓

c. It'll be a doorway into another world! ☐

d. Mysteries and horrors that you can't imagine in your wildest dreams! ☐

3. Life is ...

a. All about love. ✓

b. Hard but rewarding. ✓

c. A carnival! ☐

d. Dangerous - you always have to watch your back! ☐

4. You receive a mysterious email, telling you to expect a surprise visitor later that day. Who do you hope it is?

a. Your boyfriend with a huge bunch of flowers and tickets to your fave band! ✓

b. An old friend you haven't seen for years. You have some deep and serious catching up to do! ☐

c. The producer of a hit show, asking you to take the lead role in his new production. ✓

d. Someone who will lead you into a dark and dangerous mystery! ☐

News

5. Your best friend tells you that she doesn't like your new outfit. How do you react?

a. You totally panic. You're meeting your boyfriend in half an hour and now you find out that you look like a fashion disaster! You're gonna have to hit the mall fast! ☐

b. You listen to what she has to say. If you think she's right, you go and change the outfit. But sometimes fashion is about personal taste, right? ✔

c. You just laugh at her. If she doesn't like your style, that's just because it's way too fashion-forward for her! ☐

d. What's she talking about? It's black, and it looks just like all your other black outfits! ☐

6. You're scorchin' on the dance floor of a club with your friends, when a loud alarm goes off. What do you do?

a. Scream and panic, then run in the wrong direction and get lost. Your boyfriend rescues you just in time! ☐

b. You keep your head and make your way quietly to the exit. There's nothing to be scared of. ✔

c. Calm all your frightened friends down by getting them to join in a song! By the time the authorities arrive, the entire club is singing and dancing in the street outside! ☐

d. You slip through a side door to the basement. Someone set that alarm off on purpose and you're gonna find out who! ✔

7. What's your idea of the perfect background scene?

a. Sunset over a secluded beach, with birdsong in the air! ☐

b. A windswept moor, with wild horses in the distance. ☐

c. A fairground, full of people, colours and laughter! ✔

d. A Paris street at night, gleaming with rain in the moonlight. ✔

8. Who would you pick to write the soundtrack of a film about your life?

a. McFly. ☐

b. James Blunt. ☐

c. Kylie Minogue. ☐

d. Avril Lavigne. ✔

Mostly As - You're fun, outgoing and lighthearted, and you have lots of friends. You should play the lead in a romantic comedy!

Mostly Bs - You're intelligent, serious and sensitive. You would win Oscars in emotional dramas!

Mostly Cs - You love anything that's outrageous and over the top! You enjoy attention and applause - you'd be fabulous in a musical!

Mostly Ds - You have a dark side, girl, and you crave excitement and adventure. You would suit tense thrillers and tangled mysteries!

Glitz 'n' Glam

They're rolling out the red carpet and it's time to strut your stuff! Use these model mannequins to design some rockin' Hollywood gowns that'll make the covers of all the hottest fashion mags. Embellish and personalise a look for each girl. Then use soft colouring pencils to complete the designs.

Hollywood Dreams

If you can't get to Hollywood, make Hollywood come to you! Every girl knows that there is nothing more fun than planning a party that everyone will be talking about afterwards!

Invitations

Send out invitations on specially designed pieces of card. You could make them look like film reel or like clapperboards! Don't forget to include the date, time and place.

Dress Code

Ask everyone to dress like movie stars from the 1930s and 1940s - Hollywood's golden age! Make sure you give them a few pointers on your invitation. The guys should wear suits and bow ties, and the girls should think totally glam, with sparkling dresses, luxurious wraps and eye-poppin' jewellery!

Hair and Makeup

Ask your best friends to come over early so that you can do your hair and makeup together! If you're going for a retro theme, try some old-style up-dos - held in place with a spritz of firm-hold hairspray! Check out some black-and-white movies for inspiration. Makeup was super-glam, with false lashes and rich, red lips.

Make an Entrance!

If you are lucky enough to find some old red carpet or thick red material, lay it down outside your house for the ultimate Hollywood entrance! Make sure there is someone checking invitations at the start of the red carpet (you don't want any of those pesky journalists sneaking in!) and tie gold and silver metallic balloons at the door.

Refreshments

Serve delicate finger foods and home-made sparkling lemonade in wide, retro-style champagne glasses! Place snacks on silver platters and arrange bowls of olives with small cocktail sticks through them.

Music

To really capture the mood, raid your 'rents music collection and play some old-time band or swing music as your guests are arriving. (You can put on the floor-fillin' hip-hop tracks when everyone has arrived!)

Movie Mad

If you're an IT hotshot, set up a TV and computer screen to play your fave old films. Turn the sound down and just let them run in the background - it'll feel like you've got some real-life film stars at your party!

Picture Perfect

You can pick up old posters and postcards of films and movie stars at markets and car boot sales. Create unique displays as temporary replacements for the pics on your walls!

Paparazzi

No glam celebrity cash is complete without photographers! Assign a couple of creative friends to snap shots of your guests enjoying the party. Make sure each dress is pictured - and ask your girl guests where their outfits came from. You can even make them into a souvenir booklet afterwards!

Accessorise

Accessories are a total must-have for any fashion-forward girl, so here's my super-stormin' guide to building up the all-time best accessories. You should never be stuck for something awesome to complete your outfit!

1

Check out your wardrobe. What are your fave outfits? Do you always wear the same old accessories with each outfit? NOT COOL! You are wasting fashion opportunities, girlfriend! You can actually make an outfit look completely different, just with a new belt, scarf or bag. So first, make a list of all your fave outfits. Note the colours, textures and styles of each garment.

2

Now make a list of your accessories. That means every bag, necklace, belt, scarf, hairclip … shame on you if they are all stuffed into a corner of a drawer! Which accessories do you have most of? Are they all the same colour or style? If any of them are worn out or broken, decide whether they can be recycled as part of something else. If not, throw them!

3

Now bring your two lists together. You'll soon see where you are lacking accessories. Do you have a ton of retro 60s smock tops but no long bead necklaces? Do you have some super-glam dresses but no sequinned purses? Check your lists against each other, and figure out where you need an accessory injection!

©MGA

Your Life!

4

Shopping time! Make a list of any charity shops, markets or car boot sales around your area. They are the best places to pick up unique pieces that have super squeal-appeal! If any of your outfits need an exact colour match, take them with you. Choose a day when you've got plenty of time and go alone - this takes time and patience! It's not as easy as buying off the rack in a shop, but this way, no one else is gonna be cramping your style by wearing the same accessories!

5

Set a budget. Don't get carried away and buy tons of stuff you'll wear once. Make a rule that you will only buy something if it will go with more than two of your outfits!

6

Don't forget that you can recycle all sorts of halfway-hot accessories. If you see a super-stylin' pendant on a fashion-disaster chain, buy it anyway. You can ditch the chain and re-thread the pendant yourself! Train yourself to look at the individual parts of items, and you will soon see that there's beauty in the weirdest places!

7

Now you've got your brand-new collection of amazing accessories, keep 'em in great condition! Jade loses hers all the time behind wardrobes and chests of drawers, under beds and even draped over lampshades! Keep your jewellery box tidy, stash your bags neatly in a drawer and hang scarves and belts from hangers in the wardrobe.

Have fun accessories hunting - I hope that you find some super-cool treasures that you'll use forever!

Sasha x

Angel's Abstract Art

It's so easy to create a simple, stunning work of art - and it's great fun too! Here's how to paint a masterpiece! An abstract painting uses shapes and colours instead of people or objects. For your very first picture, you're gonna draw rectangles. But when you've got the hang of it, you can try out all sorts of colours and shapes!

You will need:

- **Square deep-edge canvas**
- **Acrylic paint in dark blue and white.**
- **Three washable containers.**
- **Paintbrushes with springy bristles.**
- **Soft drawing pencil.**
- **Lots of rectangular objects to draw around.** Look out for some long, thin rectangle shapes and some thicker, shorter ones.

What to do:

1 Take your pencil and the largest rectangular shape. Draw around it onto the middle of the canvas. The rectangle should be narrow and tall, like a skyscraper.

2 Draw two more rectangles exactly the same size, one on either side of the first shape.

3 Now take a smaller rectangle shape and draw around it inside each of the first rectangles you drew.

Repeat step 6 with an even smaller rectangle.

Now choose some more rectangles and draw around them all over your canvas. The rectangles can be next to each other, overlap or be inside each other. But they should always be going straight up or straight across. They should never be diagonal!

Squirt some dark blue paint into the first two containers and white paint into the third container.

Add a little white paint to one of the first two containers, to make a medium blue.

Add a little bit of blue paint to the third container to make a very light blue. You should now have three different shades of blue.

Leave it to dry. Then amaze your friends with your creation!

Now you can start to paint! Your three sets of rectangles inside rectangles will look awesome using the three shades of blue. Paint one set with the darkest blue on the outside rectangle. Then paint the next set with the darkest blue on the inside rectangle!

Now you know how, you can experiment with other colours, shapes and canvases! Have fun!

Cloe x

81

Video Vogue

Part 2

Next day, Cloe got up early and grabbed her fave breakfast - a fruit smoothie and a bowl of cereal with yoghurt. Then she hopped into her car and headed out of Stilesville. She was halfway to Uptown City, cruising along with her radio blasting some off-the-hook tunes, when the car gave a sudden jerk. Then it made a loud popping sound and smoke started to pour out of the bonnet.

"Oh no, no, no!" Cloe cried, stopping the car. **"This cannot be happening!"**

Cloe glanced around, but there were no other cars around for miles. She flipped open her mobile and groaned.

"No signal!" she said. **"I don't believe it!"**

She got out of the car and started to walk around, trying to find a signal. Step by step she got further away from the car.

© MGA

She walked past some bushes and over a little hill. There was still no signal. **"What am I going to do?"** Cloe wailed aloud. Then she looked up and saw something that made her gasp in astonishment. In front of Cloe was what looked like an old, crumbling ... *castle*. One of the walls was missing and she could see inside. There were fairytale turrets and a spiral staircase that was falling to pieces. Ivy clung to the walls and white, flowering weeds were growing among the brick and stone. It was beautiful and ruined at the same time, and it looked like something straight out of a book.

Cloe stared, open-mouthed. She had never seen anything like it before, but it was as though something had brought her here for a reason.

"It's the perfect place!" she gasped. "I have to tell the others!"

© MGA

83

As soon as Cloe got a signal, she called a garage to come and fix her car. Then she drove back to Stilesville in a whirl of excitement. Her friends were in the Bratz magazine studio when she raced in and told them about the amazing venue she had discovered. **"It sounds perfect!"** said Sasha. "We have to find out who owns it, and then ask for permission to film there!" Yasmin spun her chair around to her computer and started searching the internet for information. **"Here it is!"** she said at last. "It's owned by a Mr Knight, but he has never lived there." "What's his telephone number?" asked Sasha. **"I'm on the case!"**

Fifteen minutes later, the girls were perched on their desks, listening to Sasha's side of a phone conversation. At last she put the phone down and they waited with bated breath.

© MGA

"It's all arranged," said Sasha, smiling. "Mr Knight was really helpful!"

"So we can use it?" Cloe said in excitement.

"Yes - he's glad that someone wants it for something!" Sasha explained. "It was built years ago by his great-grandfather, but it was just for show - no one ever lived there. They used to play in it when they were kids, but now it's falling down. He can't afford to repair it, but he doesn't want to knock it down either - he really loves it."

"That's really sad," said Cloe. "I wish we could do something to help."

"Right now, all we have time to do is make the video," said Sasha. "We should start right away, you guys! Meygan's gonna meet us out there. Come on, let's grab our equipment and get changed!"

The girls hurried down to Cloe's convertible. They packed their makeup bags, outfits, instruments, cameras and equipment in, and then squeezed in themselves.

"Let's hit the road!" cried Jade.

85

Cloe drove out to the castle and eagerly led her friends up to it. Jade, Sasha and Yasmin were totally staggered when they saw the fairytale building.

"This is such an extreme setting," said Jade, looking around at the crumbling walls and the creeping ivy. "You know what … this would make a scorchin' fashion-shoot background for the next issue of *Bratz* magazine!"

"You are so right, Kool Kat!" Cloe gasped. "We should definitely do that!"

"I can just imagine the sort of fashions we could model here!" said Yasmin. "It would suit ol'-style gowns with a modern, edgy twist."

"Can we think about this assignment first?" said Sasha with a laugh. "Help me unload the stuff."

They unpacked the car and set up their cameras and sound equipment.

"Hey - here's Meygan!" called Yasmin suddenly.

Their friend Meygan was
walking towards them. She looked
sassy and super-sweet in her flared jeans
and gold-and-turquoise top.
**"You look spectacular enough to be in this
video, not just filming it!"** said Jade,
hugging Meygan.
"No way!" laughed Meygan, flicking back her
auburn hair. "I'm happy to let you girls do the
singing, thanks!"
"Let's get this show on the road!" said Sasha,
who was setting up the amplifier. "We've got a
ton of work to do!"
"This place is awesome," said Meygan as she
helped to set up the equipment. "How did you
find it, Angel?"
"Total luck," said Cloe with a laugh. "I was
getting really worried that I would never find
the perfect venue, and suddenly - here it was!"

Soon, the cameras were in position and the
girls were ready for their first take. They
checked that their instruments were in
tune and then Meygan started
rolling the cameras.

© MGA

Jade, Sasha, Cloe and Yasmin were determined to make their video the best it could be. They gave each take everything they had, and the creative vibe was just as vibrant as if they were on stage, performing to an audience.

"I wonder if the other kids on our media studies class are having this much fun on their assignments," said Jade after the first take.

"Not possible!" said Sasha, playing a blastin' riff on her guitar. Meygan was buzzing with energy too, and as the music rocked the old castle, she zipped between the cameras, adjusted light and sound levels, and suggested where each girl should stand to create the hottest look for the Rock Angelz video.

"This is jumpin'!" said Sasha as they checked the film after the second take. "The colours of the outfits really stand out against the stone walls of the background!"

© MGA

"This doesn't feel like work at all," said Cloe. **"I'm having way too much fun!"**
But the girls did work very hard all day to get as many different shots and angles as they could. They were dedicated to producing the very best footage they could. They had to sing the song over and over again, but each time their performances just seemed to get better and better!
"You girls really are stars," said Meygan. "I don't know how you kept that song sounding so fresh, but even though I have heard it tons of times today, I'm still loving it!"
"That's thanks to Yasmin's inspired lyrics," said Jade.
"Not to mention Sasha's rockin' music," Cloe added.
"I think it's the energy you all pour into your work," said Meygan. "You just seem to enjoy it so much!"
"We do!" giggled Cloe. **"Come on, Meygan - it's time you joined in too!"**

© MGA

"Yes!" Yasmin insisted.
"Set the cameras to auto and join us
for one take!"
Sasha tossed a microphone to Meygan and they
began to play. Meygan joined Yasmin in the lead
vocals, and it was one of the best performances of the day!
When they finished, they all whooped and cheered.
"You have an awesome voice!" Jade told Meygan.
"That was fun," Meygan admitted. "But performing in front of you
in a crumbling old castle is very different from performing on stage to
an audience of hundreds! I could never do what you girls do. I would
still rather be behind the camera!"

The girls carried on working until the light
began to fade. At last, Meygan gave them
the thumbs up.
"That's a wrap!" she called.
"Awesome work, you guys!"
"You too!" said Yasmin,
rushing over to hug
Meygan. "We couldn't
have done it
without you!"

© MGA

90

Next day, the five girls
hooked up at the editing suite in
Stilesville Library. They watched all the
footage that Meygan had shot the day before.
"It's all so fabulous, I hate to cut any of it!" said Sasha,
flicking back her long, dark hair.
"We've got to be ruthless," said Jade. **This video is gonna
be the best of the best!"**
"And that's the attitude that makes Bratz magazine so amazing,"
Cloe agreed.
They worked all day, choosing only the most
perfect shots.
"Finished!" said Sasha as she clicked
the final button and burnt the video
to disc.
"I think it's awesome, you guys,"
said Meygan.
"Thanks to you!" said Jade. "I
would love you to be our model in
a fashion shoot out at the castle -
what do you say?"
"I say … bring it on!"
exclaimed Meygan. "That
sounds like so much fun!"
"Totally!" agreed Cloe.
"I can't wait to show the
class this spectacular
video!" said Yasmin.

On Monday morning,
everyone filed into the media studies
classroom. The other students were looking
tired, and all of them were holding DVDs.
**"I wonder if everyone is as pleased with their videos as
we are,"** whispered Cloe to Yasmin.

"Not possible!" said Yasmin with a
wide smile.

Mr Lee wheeled a large-screen TV
into the room and looked around at
the students.

"I'm really looking forward to seeing
what you all came up with - and
hearing about the problems you
encountered," he said. **"First up,
Jade, Cloe, Yasmin and Sasha!"**
The girls joined hands as their video
was put on for the class. The Rock
Angelz logo blazed across the
screen, and then there was a wide
shot of the castle. The other
students gasped when they saw
the setting.

© MGA

92

As the first bars of 'On the Edge' were heard, the camera zoomed in at super-speed to a close up of Sasha's hands on her guitar. Sasha played the first chords of the song and then the Rock Angelz launched into the first verse.

"Can't control the music, can't forget the song, When I feel the rhythm I've just gotta sing along! Livin' on the edge, feelin' wild and free! Chillin' with my girls, it's the only way to be!"

The outfits that Jade had picked really stood out on the film, and the four friends could hardly believe how professional the finished video looked!

The other kids in the class were soon singing along and clapping. There were sighs and exclamations as the video revealed more of the awesome background setting. At the end of the video, there was a huge round of applause.

©MGA

Mr Lee smiled at the girls.

"That was a great job, ladies," he said, warmly. "You really captured a wonderful sense of atmosphere, and the camera shots and angles were perfect. Well done - I'm giving you an A!"

"Yes!" cheered the girls, joining in a group high five. **"So cool!"**

They eagerly watched the other students' videos and cheered loudly for each one. They were all awesome! Best of all, at the end of the lesson, Mr Lee promised that they wouldn't have any more homework for a week!

"I thought it was gonna be horrible to have to work all weekend," said Jade, as they left the classroom. "But it was the best fun!"

"**Totally,**" agreed
Sasha. "We learned tons about
how to make a music video, and we created a super-stylin' promo
video for the Rock Angelz!"
"And we found a super-stylin' new fashion-shoot location," added Cloe.
"I've been thinking about that," said Yasmin. "I bet that we could help Mr Knight
turn the castle into a location for all sorts of things - fashion shoots … videos …
even movies!"
"**You're right!**" Sasha exclaimed. "It might even help him to earn enough money
for a few repairs."
"Not too many, though!" Jade laughed. "I kinda dig the crumbling, ruined
look of the place - it gives it a great edge."
"**Just like our music video!**" said Cloe.

Chinese Horoscopes

First, figure out which animal's year you were born in!

Year of the Horse:	1990 - 1991
Year of the Sheep:	1991 - 1992
Year of the Monkey:	1992 - 1993
Year of the Rooster:	1993 - 1994
Year of the Dog:	1994 - 1995
Year of the Pig:	1995 - 1996
Year of the Rat:	1996 - 1997
Year of the Ox:	1997 - 1998
Year of the Tiger:	1998 - 1999
Year of the Rabbit:	1999 - 2000
Year of the Dragon:	2000 - 2001
Year of the Snake:	2001 - 2002

Rat

You're clever and witty, and your natural charm makes you a great friend. But sometimes you can be a bit sharp-tongued too! You should be crushing on someone with a Dragon or a Monkey sign.

Ox

You are super-dependable and affectionate, and you can achieve anything that you put your mind to - a born leader! You can turn stubborn when others are pushing you around. You should be crushing on someone with a Snake or a Rooster sign.

Tiger

You are confident and brave, and you are often the leader in a group. You're totally passionate but sometimes you can be a bit of a drama queen! You should be crushing on someone with a Horse or a Dog sign.

©MGA

There are tons of awesome, fascinating cultures and beliefs all over the world. Yasmin has been checking out Chinese astrology for a magazine article. What does the year you were born say about you?

Rabbit

You're popular, kind and romantic, but you're a bit scared of arguments so you'll do anything to avoid a fight! You should be crushing on someone with a Sheep or a Pig sign.

Dragon

You are generous, warm and powerful, and you have a fantastic lucky streak! Sometimes you can be a lil' intolerant though, so make sure you take time out for kindness. You should be crushing on someone with a Monkey or a Rat sign.

Snake

You think before you speak and you're intelligent and careful. You're a hard worker and you are gentle and charming - you just need to learn to believe in yourself! You should be crushing on someone with a Rooster or an Ox sign.

Horse

You're always buzzin', girl, and you love activity and freedom. Your energy is infectious, but you can be a bit impatient sometimes. You should be crushing on someone with a Dog or a Tiger sign.

Sheep

You're creative, thoughtful and sometimes a bit of a daydreamer! You love to look and feel good, but you value your friends above everything! You should be crushing on someone with a Rabbit or a Pig sign.

Monkey

You love fun, energy and excitement - you are a total party animal! You're also a great listener, but you can be a bit of a klutz sometimes! You should be crushing on someone with a Rat or a Dragon sign.

Rooster

You're practical and you care about the details, so you are a bit of a perfectionist - especially about your fashions. You are super-loyal, but don't forget to listen to your heart as well as your head! You should be crushing on someone with a Snake or an Ox sign.

Dog

You are loyal, sensitive and honest, and you get a kick out of being active. You really take things to heart - sometimes a bit too much! Learn to relax a little. You should be crushing on someone with a Tiger or a Horse sign.

Pig

You have fabulous taste, great manners and a generous streak a mile wide. You care about your friends and family and you would do anything to make them happy. Just make sure you think about your needs too! You should be crushing on someone with a Rabbit or a Sheep sign.

Funky Feet

Puzzling Passions

G	N	I	T	I	R	W	P	M	A
R	M	U	S	I	C	J	X	H	Y
U	Z	R	V	B	S	K	O	O	B
O	G	N	I	C	N	A	D	L	S
M	O	V	I	E	S	V	M	I	L
A	Q	W	P	T	O	T	N	D	A
L	Y	T	I	R	A	H	C	A	M
G	T	U	H	A	Q	E	P	Y	I
N	E	I	F	A	S	H	I	O	N
V	J	S	D	N	E	I	R	F	A

Animals   Dancing   Holiday
               Fashion   Movies   done ✓
Hobbies   Friends   Music
Charity   Glamour   Writing

Photo Fan!

You will need:

Thick black paper from your
local craft shop.
Thick card.
Your fave fabric.
Fabric glue.
Hole punch.
Ribbon in your fave colour.
Photo corners.

What to do:

1

On a piece of paper, draw a simple shape. If
shoes are your thing, draw a stylin'
platform. If you love bags, draw a super-
cute handbag. The shape should be as big
as possible, but no larger than your black
paper. It should have one straight edge -
this will be the spine of your album.

2

Trace the shape onto your black paper and
cut out as many copies as you can. These
are the pages of your album.

3

Trace the shape onto your card. Cut out
two copies, slightly bigger than your paper.
These are the front and back covers of your
album.

If you've got tons of awesome photos and nowhere to put them, here's the solution. Create your very own totally fashion-forward photo albums!

4

Use your fabric glue to cover your two cardboard shapes in your fave fabric.

5

6

Now all you have to do is fill your album with stylin' snaps!

Punch holes in the pages and cover. Then thread them together with matching ribbon and tie in a double bow.

©MGA

Chime Time

You will need:

- Chime objects.
- A line to hang the chimes, such as fishing line or string.
- A circle or square of thick cardboard with holes punched in it around the edge. (Or, if your 'rents are into DIY, you could ask them to drill holes in a piece of wood instead.)
- A length of thick string or thin chain.

What to do:

1

Gather materials for your chimes from around the house, or from car boot sales, market stalls and jumble sales. Check out anything that's made from hollow metal or wood. You could even combine really unexpected objects like old tools or kitchen utensils.

2

Decorate your chimes. You could paint them all the same colour, or leave some of them natural. Try creating a riot of rich colours for an awesome summer wind chime!

Follow these easy steps to create your own awesome wind chime. Then hang it in your window for some super~soothin' sounds – taken straight from the air!

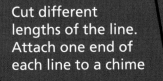

Cut different lengths of the line. Attach one end of each line to a chime

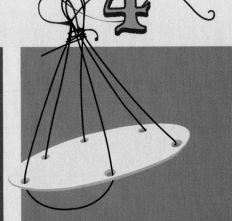

Loop the thick string or thin chain through the holes in the cardboard or wood. Tie or link them together above. This is how you will hang up your wind chime.

Tie the chimes all around the edges of the plate. They should hang at different lengths.

Hang up your wind chime and wait for the breeze to make music!

Tip: Make wind chimes for all your friends, decorated in their fave colours!

©MGA

Cloe's Makeup Tips

Think of your face as a canvas and you will soon be creating glamorous works of art! I love experimenting with different makeup looks. These suggestions will help to complete the awesome fashion styles that Jade talks about on page 54.

Sorceress

For this look, you should choose deep, dramatic neutrals that will magically make you stand out in a crowd.

1. Start off with your lipstick - a deep rose pink with a luscious satin finish. You will use this colour to build up the rest of your makeup look. Slick on a couple of coats for an opulent look.
2. Choose a cream blusher in a shade of rose that matches your lipstick, then use your fingers to blend it in. Apply it to the apples of your cheeks, and be sparing - the sorceress look is understated glamour!
3. Now it's time to make your eyes look magical! First, choose a medium neutral cream eyeshadow and sweep it over your eyelid.
4. Next, take a thinner brush and a dark neutral shade. Apply this to your lash line with the edge of the brush. Repeat this under your lower eyelashes.

Goddess

If you're gonna look like a goddess, your makeup needs to be picture perfect! Pick out vibrant, shimmering colours in gold and bronze.

1. Choose a dusky rose cream blush and apply it to your cheeks to give yourself a heavenly glow.
2. Brush a light brown shade over your eyelid, from your lash line to your brow bone.
3. Use a flat brush to sweep a dark brown eyeshadow from the inside corner of the eye across the eyelid to the outside. Make sure that the brush is loaded with eyeshadow.
4. Finally, highlight your stunning eyes with a gold shade above and below the lash lines.
5. Choose a shimmering, silky lip gloss to complete your look.

Gypsy

The gypsy look is natural and simple - you should look fresh and pretty without seeming to be made up!

1. Brush a skin-coloured shade of cream shadow over your eyelid.
2. Using a thin brush, gently sweep a light brown or pale gold shade above and close to your eyelashes.
3. Slick a transparent lip gloss over your lips.
4. Choose a cream blush in a pink shade that matches your own natural colouring. Apply it to your cheeks just enough too give a faint glow.

Super-heroine

This look requires medium neutral shades for a stylin' city look!

1. Pick a pale pink cream blush and gently apply it to the apples of your cheeks, blending with your fingertips.
2. Brush a pale, barely-there shade over your whole eyelid, using cream eyeshadow.
3. Now sweep a light brown shade over your lid using the flat side of the brush.
4. Apply a brown eyeliner using a pen liner.
5. Finally, slick a layer of lipstick on in a peachy shade and you're ready to go!

You look totally awesome! *Cloe x*

©MGA

Moreish Cheese Straws

These snacks are perfect to munch while you're watching a great movie!

Ingredients

100g butter
100g plain flour
150g extra strong cheddar cheese, grated
1 egg yolk
Cayenne pepper and black pepper
Rolling pin
Large baking tray, greased with butter or oil and lined with greaseproof paper.
An adult to help you out.

Get cooking!

1. Preheat the oven to 220ºC (gas mark 7).

2. Sieve the flour into a bowl. Add the cheese and sprinkle in some pepper. Mix the ingredients together.

3. Rub the butter into the mixture with the tips of your fingers, until the mixture looks like breadcrumbs.

4. Stir in the egg yolk and then pat the mixture together until it becomes a ball of dough.

5. Dust flour over your work surface and rolling pin. Then roll out the dough into a square shape, about half a centimetre thick.

6. Ask an adult to help you cut the dough into strips. It's up to you how big you want your straws to be!

7. Put the strips onto the baking tray and bake until they are golden brown (about 6-8 minutes).

Heavenly Hot Chocolate

Smoothies are fabulous, but sometimes you just totally crave a big mug of hot chocolate! To make your guests feel cosy and warm, serve rich, creamy hot chocolate in large mugs. Top them off with a squirt of cream and a 99 flake!

Get busy in the kitchen and whip up these divine dishes. Then invite some friends over, settle down in front of your fave movie and enjoy!

Movie Star

These delicious biscuits will make your guests feel like stars!

Get cooking!

1. Preheat the oven to 180°C (gas mark 4).

2. As your 'rents to help you put the flour, sugar and butter into a blender and mix it all together.

3. Add the eggs and keep blending until the mixture has turned into dough. Ask your 'rents to give you a hand if you have never done this before.

4. Dust flour over your work surface and rolling pin. Then roll out the biscuit dough until it is about half a centimetre thick.

5. Cut out your star-shaped biscuits and put them onto the baking trays.

6. Bake the biscuits for 15 minutes and then put them on a wire rack to cool.

7. Use your icing pen to write your guests' names on the biscuits, or draw an outline of icing in the shape of a star.

Ingredients

450g plain flour
225g sugar
225g butter or margarine
2 eggs
Icing
Rolling pin
Star-shaped biscuit cutter
Large baking trays, greased with butter or oil
Icing pen
An adult to help you out.

Drinks Drama

Use champagne glasses to serve glamorous, colourful fruit drinks. Serve sparkling grape juice, or add your fave fruit juice to lemonade for some fizzy fun! Decorate drinks with paper umbrellas and glass stirrers.

©MGA

Holiday

When you are going on an aeroplane for a long journey, make sure you know how to pack your hand luggage! There are tons of things you might need while you're on board.

The cabin crew will give you drinks and food, but there are still some items that are gonna make you feel totally relaxed for the long flight!

Choose a super-stylin' bag and make sure it's the right size (ask your 'rents or check on the airline's website). Then lay everything you want to pack out on your bed. Make sure that you only pack what you are actually going to use!

Planner

Book or magazines - If you can't sleep, make sure you have something super-gripping to read! If you're close to the end of your book, take two.

MP3 player - Make sure your battery is charged up and you have your earphones with you.

Notebook and pen - You might get inspired on the flight and have a rockin' idea for a story, a dress design or even a song. Make sure you have somewhere to write it down before you forget it!

Pashmina or large wrap - It can get chilly on a plane, so take your warmest wrap or a cosy, stylin' jumper.

Eye mask - Sure, the airline gives you one, but it's from the fashion dark ages! Make sure you look super-stylin' in your sleep.

Toothbrush - Even if you're not allowed to take toothpaste on board the flight, brushing your teeth with water will make you feel fresher!

Flannel - Give your face a zinging wash before you go to sleep - it'll freshen your skin and make you feel more relaxed.

Earplugs - They might not be the coolest look you've ever experimented with, but they will help you to get a good night's sleep and wake up looking utterly gorgeous. Just don't forget to take them out afterwards!

Make sure that your travelling clothes are comfortable, stylin' and simple. Looking good when you arrive will get your holiday off to a fabulous start!

Have an awesome year, and remember – you're stunning, you're stylin', and we're best friends forever!

Cloe x
Jade x
Yasmin x Sasha x
Meygan x

Pages 18~19

7	5	9	1	6	4	3	8	2
1	6	3	2	8	7	9	5	4
4	2	8	9	3	5	6	7	1
6	9	2	3	5	1	8	4	7
5	7	1	6	4	8	2	9	3
3	8	4	7	2	9	1	6	5
9	1	6	5	7	3	4	2	8
2	4	5	8	1	6	7	3	9
8	3	7	4	9	2	5	1	6

1	7	3	4	6	8	5	9	2
9	4	2	1	5	3	6	7	8
5	6	8	2	7	9	4	1	3
4	8	1	3	9	6	2	5	7
2	3	7	8	4	5	1	6	9
6	5	9	7	1	2	8	3	4
8	1	5	9	2	7	3	4	6
3	9	4	6	8	1	7	2	5
7	2	6	5	3	4	9	8	1

8	9	4	1	7	3	2	5	6
5	3	1	4	6	2	8	7	9
7	6	2	8	5	9	3	1	4
2	4	7	6	8	5	9	3	1
3	8	6	9	1	7	4	2	5
1	5	9	2	3	4	6	8	7
4	1	8	5	2	6	7	9	3
6	7	5	3	9	8	1	4	2
9	2	3	7	4	1	5	6	8

4	8	7	1	6	5	9	2	3
9	6	5	3	8	2	4	7	1
2	3	1	4	7	9	6	8	5
8	1	4	6	2	7	5	3	9
7	5	9	8	1	3	2	4	6
6	2	3	5	9	4	7	1	8
5	4	6	2	3	1	8	9	7
1	9	8	7	4	6	3	5	2
3	7	2	9	5	8	1	6	4